HOW TO GAIN CONTROL OF YOUR FINANCES

"A generous man will prosper."
—PROVERBS 11:25

STAN TOLER

wesleyan
publishing
house

Indianapolis, Indiana

CONTENTS

You have heard the reports. You have read the stats. You have experienced it for yourself. Americans are drowning in consumer debt. There is a good chance that either you or someone you know has filed for bankruptcy. Sometimes there are extenuating circumstances or uncontrollable events that cause a person to have severe financial difficulties, but most of the time, our financial insecurity is a result of our decisions and unwillingness to live on less than we earn. In chapter 5 of *Total Quality Life*, it says that "43 percent of American families spend . . . $1.22 . . . for every dollar earned" (p. 67). Someone has said that families today want in three years what their parents accumulated in thirty years.

The purpose for spending six weeks studying finances is not to add to your guilt. Quite the contrary! The goal of the next six weeks is to encourage you to seek total quality life by pursuing financial freedom and security. Financial security has nothing to do with the size of your bank account, and everything to do with the size of your faith in God. Total quality finance begins when we place our complete trust in God.

DAY 1

※

MATTHEW 6:25–34

It's ironic that the phrase "In God We Trust" is stamped on U.S. currency when many people place their trust in money rather than God.

At first glance, today's passage seems to be about worry in general. However, a closer look reveals that it warns against worrying about things money can buy. Jesus said, "So do not worry, saying, 'What shall we eat?' or 'What shall we drink?' or 'What shall we wear?'" (v. 31). We can assume Jesus would have included worrying about where you will live as well. Jesus says that people who worry about such things, instead of trusting in God, are acting like "pagans" (v. 32). Instead, we are to "seek first his kingdom and his righteousness" (v. 33), and as we trust him, he will take care of all that other stuff we so often worry about. "Therefore do not worry about tomorrow, for tomorrow will worry about itself. Each day has enough trouble of its own" (v. 34).

Type these verses (vv. 25–34) on a sheet of paper and stick them to your refrigerator. It will serve as a daily reminder that your trust should be in God and nothing else. Seek the things of God first, and trust him to provide everything else.

QUESTIONS FOR REFLECTION

1. On a scale of one to ten, one being bankruptcy and ten being complete financial security, where would you place your present economic situation? Why did you answer the way you did? What do you need to do to improve your situation?

2. Have you ever added up all your credit card debt? If not, do so and then spend some time in prayer asking God for wisdom, strength, and direction.

3. What is one thing that really stood out to you in today's Scripture reading?

PRAYER FOR TODAY

Dear God, please give me your wisdom and understanding as I begin this study on finances. Show me where I am placing my trust, and grant me the grace to rest completely in your provision for me. In the strong name of Jesus I pray. Amen.

DAY 2

1 TIMOTHY 6:17–19

Wealth can be a blessing or a curse. It all depends on your motives for making wealth and what you do with it once you have it. If God does bless you with wealth, Paul's admonishment to you is to be cautious. If you are wealthy in this life, Paul says "not to be arrogant" (v. 17). The Greek word translated *arrogant* means to have an exalted opinion of oneself. It is easy for the wealthy to think or act superior to others. It's tempting for some people to treat the wealthy differently, feeding their attitude of superiority. This type of attitude is futile because "wealth . . . is so uncertain" (v. 17). Even the wealthy need to "put their hope in God" (v. 17). The rich need to trust in God as much, if not more than, the poor. As stated earlier, financial security has nothing to do with the size of your bank account and everything to do with the size of your faith in God.

Paul goes on to say that the rich need to be known, not for their wealth, but for their good deeds and generosity (v. 18). The principle is quite simple: If God has blessed you, you have been blessed to be a blessing. Your wealth is not for you to hoarde, but for you to use to honor God by being kind and charitable. Unlike riches, which are uncertain, good deeds and generosity are a solid and secure investment for eternity. Furthermore, a life lived out of kindness and generosity is the secret to "life that is truly life" (v. 19). Doesn't that sound like total quality life?

QUESTIONS FOR REFLECTION

1. Why do you think it is so tempting for the wealthy to be arrogant, thinking they are superior to others? How does the way society treats wealthy people contribute to this attitude of superiority?

2. Why do you think Paul said that "wealth . . . is so uncertain" (v. 17)? Have you or someone you know experienced this truth?

3. How can good deeds and generosity create "life that is truly life" (v. 19)?

PRAYER FOR TODAY

My Father, thank you for supplying my needs and giving me so many of my wants. I recognize that all I have comes from you and that I need to use what you have given me to be a blessing to others. Lord, teach me what it means to be kind and generous. In Jesus' name I pray. Amen.

DAY 3

You may have heard someone say something like this: "Don't tell me what is important to you; show me your checkbook, and I will tell you what is important to you." If this saying is true, what is the most important thing in your life?

We too easily spend time and energy collecting stuff that quickly becomes broken or rusted. Brand new cars depreciate the moment you turn the key. Clothes go out of style. In the process of moving, you carefully pack up important items but never unpack some of them again. How important are they really?

It is for these reasons Jesus told us not to collect stuff here on earth, but to "store up for yourselves treasures in heaven" (vv. 19–20). Temporal things have temporary value. Eternal things have eternal value. This is a hard lesson to learn, which is why Jesus said, "For where your treasure is, there your heart will be also" (v. 21). That sounds a lot like "show me your checkbook, and I will tell you what is important to you."

At first glance, the next two verses (vv. 22–23) seem out of place. But look closer; these two verses set up what Jesus says in verse 24. Jesus switches analogies from the heart to the eyes, but the emphasis is still the same. A disciple of Jesus has to focus on God and God alone, and what you focus on will determine your direction. Thus, "No one can serve two masters. Either he will hate the one and love the other, or he will be devoted to the one and despise the other. You cannot serve both God and money" (v. 24).

There are two treasures, two visions, and two masters. And so a choice has to be made. A disciple of Jesus cannot have it both ways. Temporal things, like money and stuff, while they may have their place in life, are to never have first place in your life. Your focus cannot be divided. You must invest in the eternal, walk in the light, and serve God alone. What choice have you made?

QUESTIONS FOR REFLECTION

1. What do you think are some examples of treasures on earth and treasures in heaven? How would you explain the difference to someone else?

2. What do you think it means to say, "Where your treasure is, there your heart will be also" (v. 21)?

3. Why can't a follower of Jesus serve both God and money? Have you tried to do both in the past? What was the result?

PRAYER FOR TODAY

Dear Jesus, sanctify my life so that I may have an undivided devotion to you. In your name I pray. Amen.

DAY 4

PROVERBS 3, 8, 11, 13, 21, 22, 28

D on't count your chickens before they hatch." "A penny saved is a penny earned." "Money can't buy you happiness." "A fool and his money are soon parted."

These folk sayings, plus hundreds more, teach us a lot about finances. However, a better teacher than folk sayings is the Bible, especially the book of Proverbs.

For our Scripture readings today, we are going to take a tour through the book of Proverbs, which has a lot of practical advice about money.

Proverbs 3:9–10. The most important biblical principle about finances is to honor God with the first portion of what you earn. When you honor him, he promises to provide for you. There is no such promise if you do not honor him. (Tithing will be discussed in day five of this week.)

Proverbs 8:11. In the first two chapters of Proverbs, the writer personifies wisdom. Based on all the Bible teaches, it is safe to say that the person of wisdom is Jesus. John refers to Jesus as the *Logos* (Word, logic, or wisdom) of God (John 1:1). In Proverbs 8:11, the writer speaks of wisdom as a trait rather than a person. However, since having wisdom is impossible without a personal relationship with Jesus Christ, pursuing a relationship with and trusting him is more valuable than the most valuable thing on earth.

Proverbs 11:4. While wealth may have some benefits in this life, when a person stands before God, their wealth will not purchase one extra eternal benefit.

Proverbs 13:7. How often have you seen the truth of this proverb lived out? It is a lack of integrity that causes people to be someone they are not. Whatever your economic situation, be true to what God has called you to be.

Proverbs 13:22. You can't take it with you. Whatever you accumulate on earth will be left to those who follow you. Some people will deserve your inheritance; others will not.

Proverbs 21:5. Planning for financial security through budgeting, saving, and investing is better than not planning at all. Planning may not guarantee financial security, but not doing so guarantees financial insecurity.

Proverbs 21:20. A wise person knows how to manage his or her resources. A fool lives only for the moment and wastes all of his or her resources.

Proverbs 22:7. If you do not control debt, debt will control you, making you its slave.

Proverbs 28:6. Jesus expounds on this truth in the story of the rich man and Lazarus found in Luke 16:19–31. It is far better to be poor and right with God than rich and far away from him.

Proverbs 3:5–6. Even though these verses come early in Proverbs, I wanted you to read them last. The bottom line to wealth, health, and happiness—total quality life—is trusting God in all things and for all things. As we trust in him, he will guide and direct us. What a great promise!

QUESTIONS FOR REFLECTION

1. Of all the proverbs you read today, which one stands out the most to you? Why?

2. What are three lessons you learned or were reminded about during today's readings?

3. What do you know about money now that you wish you would have known when you graduated from college or began your first job?

PRAYER FOR TODAY

Dear Father, thank you so much for the great insight found in Proverbs. I pray you will give me the courage to take what I have read and learned and implement it into my financial life. Help me to seek your wisdom in this and every area of my life. In Jesus' name I pray. Amen.

DAY 5

❦

MALACHI 3:6–12

There are thirty-eight parables recorded in the Gospels, and money is a key issue in sixteen of them. In the Gospels, one out of every ten verses discusses money. In the Bible, there are five hundred verses on prayer, less than five hundred verses on faith, and over two thousand verses on money and materialism.

How you use and spend your money is a sign of your trust in God, and a huge aspect of that trust is what you do with the first 10 percent of what you earn. Do you tithe?

Tithing is taught in both the Old and New Testaments. Abraham gave 10 percent of all he had to Melchizedek, king of Salem and priest of Almighty God (Gen. 14:18–20), and this was before the law of tithing was given (Lev. 27:30). Jesus talked about money more than any other single issue. Paul changed the standard of tithing from 10 percent to "what he has decided in his heart to give" (2 Cor. 9:6–7). Many people can give more than 10 percent, but everyone should give at least 10 percent.

The basic principle behind tithing is stewardship. All you have has been given to you by God. He owns it all, not just the first 10 percent. Tithing acknowledges that truth. Malachi made it clear that when you do not tithe, you are robbing from God and are in danger of living under a curse (Mal. 3:9).

Your tithe is to be brought to the "storehouse" (v. 10), a reference to the temple or local church. God then says, "Test me in this" (v. 10). When I tithe, God causes the 90 percent I have remaining to go further than the 100 percent I would have had if I did not tithe. If you don't believe me, try it for yourself. Tithe a full 10 percent over the next three months and see what happens. God will prove himself faithful to you. He may even "open the floodgates of heaven and pour out so much blessing that you will not have room enough for it" (v. 10). God doesn't promise to make you filthy rich, but he does promise to bless you beyond measure. You can't afford not to tithe.

QUESTIONS FOR REFLECTION

1. Do you tithe a full 10 percent of your gross income? Why or why not?

2. What would happen in your church if everyone gave a full tithe?

3. How do you explain God's promise of abundant blessings to those who tithe (v. 10)? How have you seen this promise at work?

PRAYER FOR TODAY

Dear God, you have already blessed me beyond measure, and what I offer to you, I offer with the knowledge that you have given me every-thing. Grant me the grace to give back to you with a gracious heart, as you have so generously given to me. In Jesus' name I pray. Amen.

CULTIVATE CONTENTMENT

Once upon a time, there was a rich industrialist who went on vacation to a remote Caribbean island. One day as he was walking down the beach, he noticed a local fisherman sitting lazily beside his boat. "Why aren't you out there fishing?" he asked.

"Because I've caught enough fish for today," replied the fisherman.

"Why don't you catch more fish than you need?"

"What would I do with them?"

"You could earn more money," was the impatient reply, "and buy a bigger and better boat, so you could go deeper in the ocean and catch more fish. You could purchase nylon nets, catch even more fish, and make more money. Soon you'd have a fleet of fishing boats and be rich like me."

After pondering what the man had said for a few moments, the fisherman asked, "Then what would I do?"

"You could sit down and enjoy life," said the industrialist.

With a big smile on his face the fisherman replied, "What do you think I am doing now?"

The topic of this week's study is cultivating contentment. Socrates is noted for saying, "Contentment is natural wealth." How much happier, peaceful, and stress free would our lives be if we learned true contentment?

DAY 1

PSALM 37:14–26

Comparing what you have with what others have makes it difficult to be content. Especially when it appears that those who do not follow God have more and are happier than those who do follow God.

It may appear that the wicked are having an easy life, but in the end, they will get what they deserve: "their swords will pierce their own hearts" (v. 15). Thus, David wrote it is far better to be content with the little you do have than to have the wealth of the wicked (v. 16).

Who are the wicked? The Hebrew word translated *wicked* can also mean "evil." Who are these wicked, evil people? Several characteristics of the wicked are given in Psalm 37, but for our study, verse 21 is critical: "The wicked borrow and do not repay."

People who are not content with what they already have often borrow money so they can have more. God describes people who borrow without intending to repay as wicked. However, people who learn contentment are like the righteous, and they "give generously" (v. 21).

Why is righteous contentment better than wicked wealth? Because God watches over the days of the "blameless" and ensures their "inheritance will endure forever" (v. 18); and even when the economy is weak and times are bad, "they will not wither" and "will enjoy plenty" (v. 19). Similar wording is given throughout the rest of the psalm, reinforcing the fact that God will take care of the righteous, while the wicked will get what is coming to them. Therefore, be content!

QUESTIONS FOR REFLECTION

1. Why do you think people like to compare what they have and don't have with what others have and don't have? Why is comparing so dangerous?

2. Do you think it is evil to borrow money and not repay the debt (v. 21)? Why, or why not?

3. How would you explain biblical contentment to someone else?

PRAYER FOR TODAY

Father, I pray for the ability to stay focused on you and not compare my life and what I have and don't have with others. I pray you will help me count my blessings and be grateful for all you have given me. Help me not be envious of the wicked. In Jesus' name I pray. Amen.

DAY 2

PHILIPPIANS 4:10–20

Contentment is being satisfied with where God has placed you and what God has given you. It is being able to say enough is enough. Contentment doesn't mean you become complacent and apathetic; neither does it mean you don't try to improve your situation. It simply means that you are committed to letting God use you where you are with what you have as a channel to bless others and build his kingdom.

The believers in Philippi loved Paul deeply, and he loved them as well. Paul was the one who brought them the gospel. He lived, taught, cried, and rejoiced with them. The church in Philippi supported Paul financially and looked forward to his visits. Paul's letter to them is his most personal in the New Testament.

Paul greatly appreciated the church's support, but he wanted to make it clear to them that he did not expect their support, nor did he ask for it out of need. He said that he had "learned to be content whatever the circumstances" (v. 11). The Greek word translated *content* means to be satisfied or self-sufficient, free from any need of help. Paul could say enough is enough because he knew ultimately it was God who would supply his needs (v. 19).

Furthermore, Paul stated he knew what it was like to have needs and to have more than enough. He knew what it was like to be hungry and to be full. Regardless of the situation, he said he had "learned the secret of being content" (v. 12). What is that secret? In 2 Corinthians 9:8, Paul wrote that it is God who is able to make sure you have "all that you need." The word translated *need* is the same word translated *content* in verses 11 and 12. Then, back in Philippians, he wrote, "I can do everything through him who gives me strength" (v. 13). The secret to contentment is recognizing that all you have comes from God, and he is the one who has promised to meet your needs. The secret to contentment is being able to say enough is enough because of your trust in God.

Philippians 4:13 is often quoted out of context. People quote this verse for motivation in sporting events, business endeavors, or undertaking a particular task that seems impossible. But in context, Paul was saying that it is Jesus Christ who gives you the ability to be content and live within your means.

Another verse often quoted out of context is Philippians 4:19. Yes, the promise is that God will meet all your needs, but in context, the promise is conditional, and that condition is generosity. When a person can say enough is enough, that person is freed to give generously. Contentment breeds generosity, which in turn produces contentment. You cannot out give God. The more you give, the more he desires to meet your needs.

QUESTIONS FOR REFLECTION

1. How would you define contentment? How would you illustrate it?

2. How would you describe the secret to contentment to someone else?

3. What do you think is the connection between contentment and generosity? Are you content? Are you generous?

PRAYER FOR TODAY

Dear Lord, thank you for your generosity and for providing for every need that I have. Grant me the faith to trust in your provision and the ability to learn contentment in every circumstance. Give me a heart of generosity that mirrors your heart. In Jesus' name I pray. Amen.

DAY 3

LUKE 3:1–14

Has following Jesus changed your life? Are you different today than you were yesterday or last year because of your faith in him?

To say John the Baptist was eccentric would be an understatement. He lived a hazardous life in the desert; he wore harsh clothes made of camel's hair; and he preached a hard message: repent for the forgiveness of your sins. Perhaps surprisingly, many people accepted John and his message with open hearts. Instead of repelling people by his uniqueness, he actually drew large crowds out to the desert to hear what he had to say. In today's Scripture reading, we get a glimpse into John's ministry and the impact it had on those who listened. His message made a difference in people's lives, and part of that difference was learning to be content.

The crowds who came to hear this eccentric preacher with an urgent message can be divided into three categories of people.

First, there were the religious people. John had strong words for them, calling them a "brood of vipers," questioning their motives for coming out to hear his message and challenging them to "produce fruit in keeping with repentance" (vv. 7–8). What God is looking for is true repentance that results in life change.

The religious crowd then asked, "What should we do then?" (v. 10). In essence, they were asking, "What is the fruit that comes from repentance?" John answered by telling them to be generous with what they had and willing to give out of their abundance to those in need

(v. 11). A person cannot be generous until they are content with what they have.

The second category of people was the sinful people. All the people were sinful, but some had the reputation of being sinners. Here, the sinful people are the "tax collectors" (v. 12). Tax collectors were detested by the people as the lowest of the low. Like the religious people, the sinners asked, "What should we do?" (v. 12). John's answer is similar to the first group in that it had to do with contentment. He said, "Don't collect any more than you are required to" (v. 13). In other words, quit extorting people for personal profit and learn to say enough is enough.

The final category of people, represented by the "soldiers" (v. 14), was the professional people. In those days, being a soldier was a good job with great benefits. Soldiers could keep whatever money they could get out of the people by rationalizing that it was for the people's own protection. The soldiers likewise asked, "What should we do?" (v. 14). And again John's answer is the same: "Don't extort money and don't accuse people falsely—be content with your pay" (v. 14).

There are many ways in which money can change your life. There are also many ways you can "produce fruit in keeping with repentance" (v. 8). But the one way John the Baptist emphasized was in the area of contentment. Has following Jesus changed your life? Are you content? The answers to both these questions go hand in hand.

QUESTIONS FOR REFLECTION

1. In what ways has following Jesus changed your life? Are you different today than you were a year ago? Have you learned to be content?

2. Of the three categories of people mentioned in today's reading (religious, sinners, professional), in which category would you place yourself? Why?

3. The questions from all three groups were similar, as was John's answer to them. Why do you think that was the case?

PRAYER FOR TODAY

Dear God, on many occasions I have asked you, "What shall I do?" Today, your answer is to learn to be content. Thank you for that answer. Please teach me what it means to be content. Grant me your spirit of contentment. In Jesus' name I pray. Amen.

DAY 4

ECCLESIASTES 5:8–20

John Rockefeller was once asked, "How much money is enough?" His answer was, "Just a little more."

If people aren't content with the first dollar they make, they will not be content with the millionth dollar they make. King Solomon, the wisest and richest man to ever live, knew the truth of that statement. In today's Scripture reading, after pursuing wealth, Solomon concluded that riches are meaningless.

Ever since the fall of man, the wealthy have oppressed the poor. Solomon told us not to be surprised when we see such things (vv. 8–9). He then went to the heart of the matter by stating, "Whoever loves money never has money enough; whoever loves wealth is never satisfied with his income. This too is meaningless" (v. 10). What would happen to our nation's economy if those words were taken to heart on Wall Street? What would happen to your personal finances if you simply memorized verse 10?

The problem with pursuing wealth is that it doesn't satisfy and leads to sleepless nights. But a person who works hard and is content with what he or she has sleeps sweetly (vv. 11–12). Sweet dreams come from recognizing there are things more important than money.

Solomon went on to say that a "grievous evil" is when people hoarde all they have, only to make themselves miserable, and then lose everything through some misfortune (vv. 13–14). In context, it is clear Solomon was talking about those who love money but are never satisfied. This is meaningless because no matter how much you make or have, you came into the world with nothing and can take nothing with you when you die (v. 15). Anyone who pursues riches in this life receives loneliness ("eats in darkness"), frustration, affliction, and anger (v. 17).

That's the bad news. The good news is that it is possible to be content and happy. Solomon stated that it is good for people to be able to enjoy the things honest work provides, "to find satisfaction in [their] toilsome labor" (v. 18). Solomon even stated that it is good for people to enjoy wealth and possessions and to be "happy in [their] work" (v. 19). The idea is contentment, and Solomon said that contentment, regardless of your economic condition, is a "gift of God" (v. 19). Instead of pursuing riches, pursue a relationship with God, and he will grant you contentment. How did Solomon define contentment? He said it is living life without regret because God has "occupied" you "with gladness of heart" (v. 20).

QUESTIONS FOR REFLECTION

1. Why do you think Solomon said pursuing riches was meaningless? In what ways do you think this is true?

2. How would you describe contentment as a gift from God?

PRAYER FOR TODAY

Dear God, I desire nothing more than to be "occupied with gladness of heart." I desire nothing more than your gift of contentment. Help me to not pursue wealth, put to pursue you. In Jesus' name I pray. Amen.

DAY 5

1 TIMOTHY 6:6–10

Martin Luther is credited with saying, "For what God gives I thank indeed. What He withholds I do not need." It is a wonderful saying to live by. Be grateful for what you do have, and if you believe in a sovereign God, be even more grateful for what you do not have.

Paul wrote a letter to a young pastor named Timothy to instruct and encourage him in his ministry. In verses 3–5 of this passage, Paul mentioned some characteristics of false teachers. A key characteristic is that they are in ministry for the money. But instead of godliness being a path to financial profit, Paul stated that "godliness with contentment is great gain" (v. 6). The phrase "great gain" is a financial term meaning "very rich." More important than financial wealth is the peace that comes from living a godly life and being content with what God has given you. Such peace is priceless.

Paul went on to say that we should be content with the basic necessities of life (v. 8). Another word for clothing is *shelter*; so if you have food, clothing, and shelter, you are blessed. If you are content with the basic necessities of life because you know they come from God, you are rich.

When we become discontent, we "fall into temptation and a trap and into many foolish and harmful desires that plunge men into ruin and destruction" (v. 9). You don't have to look far to see the truth in that verse. And so Paul warned, "For the love of money is a root of all kinds of evil. Some people, eager for money, have wandered from the faith and pierced themselves with many griefs" (v. 10). Many people have turned their back completely on God or have grown slack in their commitment to serve God because of their desire to have more and their unwillingness to be content. Paul is not condemning money. Rather, he is condemning the love of money, the constant striving for more. If you want to be truly rich, learn to be content with what you already have.

QUESTIONS FOR REFLECTION

1. What do you think "godliness with contentment is great gain" (v. 6) means? How would you explain that to someone else?

2. How is the love of money a "root of all kinds of evil"? Can you think of specific examples?

PRAYER FOR TODAY

Heavenly Father, thank you for all you have shown me about being content. Forgive me for those times I have not been content with what you have given me. Sanctify me from this day forward so that I will practice godliness and contentment, since doing so is true wealth. Thank you for all you have done. In Jesus' name I pray. Amen.

AVOID DEBT

According to the Automated Access to Court and Electronic Records (AACER) and the American Bankruptcy Institute, 1.4 million consumers filed for personal bankruptcy in 2009; an increase of 32 percent from 2008. That means roughly one in every one hundred fifty United States adults have filed for bankruptcy. A large number of bankruptcies are caused by high medical bills and other unforeseen expenditures, but a contributing factor in all bankruptcies is overextended debt on things we really do not need. The single biggest step a person can take to achieve total quality finances is to avoid debt, especially debt on things that are not needed.

DAY 1

ROMANS 13:8–14

I owe. I owe. So off to work I go." I am sure you are familiar with that rhyme; maybe you have repeated it on your way out the door in the mornings. Many Christians can appreciate what Paul says about debt in this passage but have a difficult time applying it in their own lives.

Are we really expected to live our lives with no debt except love? A key word in verse 8 is *outstanding*. Paul is not saying we should never go into debt, and the Bible does not teach we should never borrow money. What Paul is saying is that we should pay our bills on time and meet all our financial obligations. The only outstanding or unpaid debt we should have is the "continuing debt to love one another" (v. 8). So, this verse should be applied in the most literal way possible.

You can never love enough. You can never say, "I am caught up on my love for other people. I have paid my love bill for the month. I have done my good deed for the day. I don't need to love anymore." Love is the primary characteristic of a disciple of Jesus and is the only way to fulfill all the requirements of the law (vv. 8–10).

Paul goes on to say it is crucial for us to understand the importance of love because of the urgency of the day in which we live and the immediacy of the return of Christ (vv. 11–12). Thus, part of the debt of love we owe is to "behave decently . . . not think about how to gratify the desires of the sinful nature" (vv. 13–14).

Think of all the bills you have each month. Think about your mortgage and car payments and credit card requirements. Compare how much time you spend meeting your financial obligations to how much time you spend loving other people. Now, think about how much time you would have to spend on more important things— loving others—if you could cut your debt in half. It's a sobering thought, isn't it? Life would be so much more fulfilling if we could spend more time loving each other and less time stressing over debts.

QUESTIONS FOR REFLECTION

1. What do you think Paul meant when he wrote, "Let no debt remain outstanding, except the continuing debt to love one another" (v. 8)? How can you apply that verse to your life?

2. How can you know when you have loved enough? How does love fulfill all the requirements of the law?

PRAYER FOR TODAY

Heavenly Father, thank you for loving me. Help me to love you and others with all that I have. Give me the grace to be even more diligent in meeting my obligation to love you and others than I am in working to meet my financial responsibilities. In Jesus' name I pray. Amen.

DAY 2

Several years ago, a friend had a small balance on a credit card from a department store. He was hoping to pay it off completely in the next few months, and then he received a phone call from them. The representative said they had recently received a payment from him, but they were going to return the check because they had no record of him owing them anything. My friend argued with them, saying he did owe them the money, but they insisted he did not. Eventually, a supervisor jumped in the conversation and told him that, according to their records, he no longer owed them any money. He went on to explain that the simplest thing to do was to accept what he was saying and consider it a gift. And that's what my friend did.

Have you ever fantasized about your creditors calling you and saying they have decided to cancel all your debt? What would you do if that dream became a reality? Did you know that according to the Mosaic law, every seven years all debts were to be cancelled?

Can you imagine that! Every seven years, the Israelites were to cancel the debts of every other Israelite. And even though Israelites could still collect payments from non-Israelites, they were not to do so if it meant poverty for the foreigner. The idea of cancelling debts every seven years was based on the Sabbath year established in Exodus 23:10–11 and Leviticus 25:1–7. Even though we are no longer required to live by the law, the principles behind this passage are still applicable today. What are those principles?

The passage seems to apply mainly to personal loans and debts, not necessarily to business practices. I see four principles in this passage.

First, the debts we take on should be short-term. The Bible doesn't condemn borrowing money, but it does warn against it, and it teaches we are better off if we do not borrow. However, when we do borrow money, we should be able to manage our debt, pay our bills, and keep our debts short-term.

Second, never loan someone more money than you can afford to give away. This is really true when it comes to loaning to family and friends. Before you loan someone any money, in your mind and heart, set aside the money as a gift. This way, if the person pays you back, great! But if they don't or can't, you won't become resentful and bitter; you gave the money away a long time ago. If, after a while, it becomes obvious the money is not going to be repaid, go ahead and forgive the debt. No amount of money is worth ruining families and losing friends.

Third, give generously to the poor, sick, and needy in your community. Remember, if God has blessed you, he has blessed you to be a blessing to others.

Fourth, don't worry about being taken advantage of. Your responsibility is to be generous. Yes, there are people who will use and abuse you, but that is not your concern. Your concern is to be obedient to God.

Seven years from now, you may still owe someone money. Chances are that no one is going to forgive your debts. But that doesn't mean you can't forgive others, and it doesn't mean you can't be generous. "For the LORD your God will bless you as he has promised" (v. 6).

QUESTIONS FOR REFLECTION

1. Do you think forgiving debts every seven years would work in today's global economy? Why or why not? What about for you personally? Do you think this idea would be beneficial?

2. Of the four principles given in today's study, which one stands out the most to you? Which one do you think is the most important? Why?

PRAYER FOR TODAY

God, open my eyes and show me the poor, sick, and needy around me. Please grant me a generous spirit so that I can give without expecting anything in return. In Jesus' name I pray. Amen.

DAY 3

PROVERBS 6, 11, 17, 22, 23, 27, 28

The book of Proverbs has a lot to say about borrowing money and managing debt. For our Scripture reading today, let's take a journey through Proverbs, reading a handful of verses about avoiding debt.

Proverbs 6:6–8. Human beings are the only living creatures who borrow and loan money and resources to each other. All other living things must plan and save for what they need. We have much to learn from even the simplest creatures, like ants.

Proverbs 11:15; 17:18. It is better to give to the needy than to make yourself responsible for someone else's debts. It is dangerous to help someone else get a loan by putting up collateral for them.

Proverbs 11:28. There really is no such thing as financial security. Security is only found in God.

Proverbs 22:1. Money has a way of ruining people. More important than financial wealth is personal integrity. Always choose character over commercialism.

Proverbs 22:26–27. Every loan is eventually called in. If you don't manage your finances well and overextend yourself, you will lose everything, even your home.

Proverbs 23:4–5. Delayed gratification is a key to financial wealth. Don't borrow money to purchase today what you can save up and pay cash for tomorrow.

Proverbs 27:23–27. Pay attention to your portfolio. Budget wisely and save for the future. Doing so will help ensure your future needs are met.

Proverbs 28:19. Another key to financial wealth is to stick to something. A person who continually jumps from one good idea to another, one job to another, or one "once-in-a-lifetime opportunity" to another will only have a life of poverty.

Proverbs 28:20. Another word for *faithful* is *diligent* or *honorable*. A person, who faithfully goes about his or her business, fulfilling responsibilities and living an honorable life, will be blessed. A person who only wants to get rich will never be satisfied.

May God help us to apply the outstanding financial advice from Proverbs to our lives.

QUESTIONS FOR REFLECTION

1. How much money do you spend each month that is unnecessary? What can you do today to change that pattern?

2. Which proverb really stood out to you today? Why?

PRAYER FOR TODAY

Dear God, thank you for the wisdom that is found in your Word. Give me the courage and strength to apply what I have learned to my financial situation. Help me get a handle on my finances today and avoid the crush of debt. In Jesus' name I pray. Amen.

DAY 4

2 KINGS 4:1–7

What does it say about your faith when, instead of trusting God to provide, you rush to the creditors to provide? In today's Scripture reading, we read an incredible story about how God miraculously provided for a widow and her son.

The "company of the prophets" (v. 1) referred to an association or school of prophets where they would go to learn and find encouragement from other prophets. Apparently, the husband was away at such a school when he unexpectedly died. The man and his wife had considerable debt, and now that he was dead, the woman was concerned that her two boys would be sold into slavery to pay the creditors. Right away, we see the danger of debt.

Instead of rushing out to borrow more money, the widow went to Elisha for advice. Elisha asked her to look around her home for something she could sell or use to make money. The woman said a little bit of olive oil was all she had (v. 2). During ancient times, olive oil was used for food and fuel. When faced with a financial need, instead of rushing into debt, our first reaction should be to seek godly counsel and look around at the resources we have on hand that can be used to produce more income. And then, we have to allow God the opportunity to provide.

Elisha instructed the widow to collect empty jars from neighbors and, behind closed doors, pour her oil into all the jars she collected (vv. 3–4). Why did Elisha tell her to "shut the door" (v. 4)? All we can do is speculate why, but since the widow's need was private, perhaps

God wanted to provide for her privately. She and her sons were the only ones who needed to see the miracle.

The widow obeyed Elisha's instructions, and God multiplied the little she had, enabling her to sell enough oil to pay off her debts with money left over for her and her sons to live on (vv. 5–7).

What financial need is concerning you? Have you prayed about that need? Have you sought godly counsel? Is it really a need? What do you have in your house that can be sold? Have you allowed God the opportunity to meet that need? Don't let your first reaction to a financial crisis be to rush out and borrow more money, especially if it is debt that caused the crisis in the first place. Allow God the opportunity to do the impossible in your situation.

QUESTIONS FOR REFLECTION

1. What does it say about a person's faith when, instead of trusting God to provide, he or she rushes to the creditors to provide? Can you think of an example where you would have been better off trusting God to meet a need instead of adding to your debt to meet it?

2. Why do you think God wanted to meet the widow's need in private? Would it not have been better to meet the need publicly?

3. What role did the neighbors play in meeting the widow's need? What do you think is the significance of including the neighbors in the miracle?

PRAYER FOR TODAY

Dear God, I confess that in the past I have sometimes been too quick to go into debt instead of allowing you the opportunity to meet my need. Help me to be more patient and discerning in the future. I trust you to provide for me. In Jesus' name I pray. Amen.

DAY 5

LUKE 12:13–21

The more you avoid debt, the more quality of life you will enjoy. One reason many people overextend themselves financially is because they have bought the bumper sticker lie that "he who dies with the most toys wins." Our society has a way of defining success by how much you can accumulate, even if you have to borrow to get more. In today's Scripture reading, Jesus makes it clear there is far more to life than accumulating more possessions.

Thousands of people had gathered around Jesus and his disciples to hear him teach (v. 1). While he was speaking, someone interrupted him: "Teacher, tell my brother to divide the inheritance with me" (v. 13). We are not told why the brother would not divide the inheritance or even if the brother asking the question was owed any inheritance.

Jesus did not get in the middle of the family struggle, but he did take the opportunity to address the larger topic of greed. What he said runs counter to our culture's view of material possessions. Jesus said, "Watch out! Be on your guard against all kinds of greed; a man's life does not consist in the abundance of his possessions" (v. 15). Your life is more than your accumulations. What you do and do not have does not define who you are.

To get his point across, Jesus told a parable that sounds a lot like the rich industrialist described earlier in this study guide. In the parable, a farmer has some success and builds bigger barns in order to store more crops so he can purchase more stuff so he can then build bigger barns and buy even more things. His goal is to retire wealthy so he can enjoy life (vv. 16–19). Unfortunately, before he can enjoy the benefits of his greed, he dies (v. 20). Jesus then concluded, "This is how it will be with anyone who stores up things for himself but is not rich toward God" (v. 21).

You are so much more than the sum of all your possessions. It is foolish to go further into debt for things that will not last. It is far better to spend your life serving God and others. It is far greater to be a giver instead of a taker and hoarder. After you die, no one will care what kind of car you drove or the square footage of your home. What others will care about is how much you loved them and how you made a difference in their lives.

Drive down any country road and you will see huge barns that were once a sign of success, but are now empty and dilapidated, except for the wildlife living inside them. The only things that last for eternity are the things you do for God.

QUESTIONS FOR REFLECTION

1. What defines who you are?

2. Why do you think God calls the actions of the rich man in the parable foolish?

PRAYER FOR TODAY

Lord, thank you so much for this week dedicated to avoiding debt. I have been challenged, and I pray my life will be different from this day forward. Help me to find my identity in you and not in things. In Jesus' name I pray. Amen.

AVOID MATERIALISM

RECOMMENDED READING

Total Quality Life, chapter 5, pages 76–82

Does your house have a garage? How many cars can you actually park in it? Are there cars in your garage, or is it a place to store all the important stuff you have accumulated over the years? Do you rent a storage unit for the rest of your stuff you just had to have? If your garage was empty, would you be able to park your SUV and minivan there at the same time? What about that third car you own, or at least are making payments on—where do you park it? Do you have a fourth car? What about a motorcycle or boat?

Why do we have so much stuff? Why do we continue to purchase more and more and more? It's because we are products of our culture, and our culture is obsessed with materialism and commercialism. The topic for this week's study is avoiding materialism so we can achieve total quality finances.

DAY 1

COLOSSIANS 2:6–10

Materialism refers to our fixation with the importance of material objects and wealth as a sign of success and significance. Closely related to materialism is commercialism, which alludes to our society's overemphasis on profit, success, and immediate results. Both are worldly philosophies, which the Bible tells us to avoid.

As a follower of Jesus Christ, it is important for you to continue to grow and mature in your faith. Paul stated that in the same way you have "received Christ Jesus as Lord," you should "continue to live in him" (v. 6).

One way you continue through faith is by staying focused on Jesus so you will not be robbed (the meaning behind "takes you captive") "through hollow and deceptive philosophy" (v. 8). In Paul's day, one of the deceitful philosophies Christians had to battle was Gnosticism, the belief that higher, supernatural knowledge was necessary to be like Jesus. According to Gnostics, Jesus was not born God but became God-like through this higher knowledge. Likewise, you and I can become God-like through these hidden mysteries that only Gnostic philosophers can teach us. This is why Paul stated, "For in Christ all the fullness of the Deity lives in bodily form, and you have been given fullness in Christ, who is the head over every power and authority" (vv. 9–10). Throughout Paul's letters and early church history, many of the controversies and church splits were over Gnostic teachings.

Today, a "hollow and deceptive philosophy" (v. 8) that is harming churches and hurting believers is the belief that happiness, and even

God's blessing, is equated with material things. In other words, the more you have, the more God has blessed you and the more he loves you. Materialism is as dangerous to Christians today as Gnosticism was to the Christians during the first century. Swallowing the lie of materialism can ruin a person's faith. At all costs, you and I should avoid materialism and commercialism. They are deceitful philosophies that can severely damage our spiritual growth.

QUESTIONS FOR REFLECTION

1. How would you define materialism? How would you describe the dangers of materialism to someone else?

2. In what ways are materialism and commercialism "hollow and deceptive" (v. 8) philosophies?

3. What can you do this week in an attempt to avoid materialism?

PRAYER FOR TODAY

Lord God, transform me so that my thoughts and feelings reflect my faith in you more than my culture. Guard my mind and heart and help me to discern your way. In Jesus' name I pray. Amen.

DAY 2

1 JOHN 2:15–17

In the late 1800s and early 1900s, German sociologist Max Weber wrote and taught that three things determined a person's social ranking in Western, industrialized societies, including the United States. The first was class position (upper, middle, lower class), which was mainly based on a person's economic situation. Second was what he called social prestige, which was primarily based on a person's occupation. For example, our society tends to treat medical doctors differently than custodians. Third was power, which referred to a person's ability to influence others. Usually these three things go together. People with prestigious jobs generally make more money, buy more possessions, and influence more people. Thus, according to Weber, our society ranks its members based on position (determined by possessions), prestige, and power.

According to today's Scripture reading, Weber was right; and as followers of Jesus, we are to avoid this type of worldly thinking. John's admonition about not loving the world does not mean we should not love and protect the beauty of creation. Rather, he was referring to the world's way of thinking and behaving. John is telling us not to love the philosophies and value systems that characterize people who are not followers of God. Following Jesus is a countercultural way of life.

According to John, the world's value system is based on three things: "the lust of the flesh, the lust of the eyes, and the pride of life" (v. 16 NIV 2011). Christ followers are not to love those things because they are not of or from God, but are of the world and come from it (v. 16). "Lust of the flesh" (NIV 2011) refers to things that make you feel good. Applied to materialism, this means if you think something will make you feel good, then purchase it. The more you buy, the better you will feel. "Lust of the eyes" (NIV 2011) refers to things that make you look good. Applied to materialism, if you think a particular car, house, or style of clothes will make you look good to others, then gratify yourself and buy it. "Pride of life" (NIV 2011) refers to things that make you believe you have arrived and deserve all the stuff you have accumulated. Applied to materialism, this means if you work hard, then you should indulge yourself with what money can buy. Go ahead and gratify your desires. You deserve it.

Do you see the connection between what the Bible says and what Max Weber, a secular humanist, taught? The world's value system ranks people into a hierarchy based on position and possessions ("lust of the flesh," NIV 2011), prestige ("lust of the eyes," NIV 2011), and power ("pride of life," NIV 2011). Our value system and way of thinking as disciples of Jesus should be radically different.

QUESTIONS FOR REFLECTION

1. How quickly were you able to place yourself in the category of upper class, middle class, and lower class? How comfortable were you in doing so?

2. How would you describe "the lust of the flesh, the lust of the eyes, and the pride of life" (v. 16 NIV 2011) to someone else? Can you give specific examples of each?

3. As a follower of Jesus, how do you think your value system should be different from the world's? Can you be specific?

PRAYER FOR TODAY

Dear Jesus, help me to see through the world's way of living, thinking, and acting. Give me the strength to be countercultural. Teach me to treat everyone equally without placing people in categories and assigning labels. May your will be done in my life. In Jesus' name I pray. Amen.

DAY 3

❦

MARK 4:1–20

There is a bumper sticker that reads, "Crime doesn't pay . . . and neither does farming." Although there are some wealthy farmers, many barely make enough money to support their families. So, in our culture, it is a little difficult to comprehend Jesus using a story about farming to discuss the effects of materialism. But farming in Jesus' day could lead to great wealth.

In ancient Palestine, unlike today, sowing preceded plowing. The farmer in Jesus' story wasn't wasting seed; he was sowing in a broadcasting style, scattering seed all around him, unconcerned with where the seed fell. Later, he would come back with a plow and turn the dirt over, burying the seed. Jesus said that during this process of sowing and then plowing, some of the seed fell on the path or rocky places, and some became entangled with thorns. But much of the seed fell on good soil "and produced a crop, multiplying thirty, sixty, a hundred times" (v. 8).

Later that evening, Jesus' disciples asked him the meaning of the story. Jesus said the story was about the kingdom of God and the different ways in which people received the message (vv. 10–13). The seed is the word or message Jesus proclaimed, and that message was, "The kingdom of God is near. Repent and believe the good news!" (Mark 1:15). The farmer was Jesus himself, but also anyone who proclaimed his message. The soil represented people's receptivity to Jesus' message—their hearts. Some people's hearts are hard. They hear the message of Jesus but reject it outright (4:14–15). Other people's hearts are shallow. They hear the message and initially accept it, but the moment following Jesus becomes uncomfortable, their faith withers and dies (vv. 16–17). Fortunately, many people's hearts are good soil. They hear Jesus' message, accept it, obey it, live it out every day, and produce bountiful crops (v. 20).

There is also a part of the story that deals with the danger of materialism. There is the hard heart, the shallow heart, and the good heart. But there is also the overcrowded heart. Many people hear Jesus' message and initially accept it, but then life gets in the way and chokes them spiritually. Jesus says three things choke the spiritual life out of a person—worries, wealth, and wants. And all three are the result of materialism. Jesus said, "Still others, like seed sown among thorns, hear the word; but the worries of this life, the deceitfulness of wealth and the desires for other things come in and choke the word, making it unfruitful" (vv. 18–19).

As believers in Jesus Christ, we need to avoid materialism, because the more stuff we have, the more worries we'll have; the more wealth, the more problems; and the more wants, the more jealousy. In essence, materialism breeds greed, and greed is never satisfied.

QUESTIONS FOR REFLECTION

1. Is your heart toward the message of Jesus hard, shallow, over-crowded, or good? Why did you answer the way you did?

2. In what ways does materialism overcrowd a person's heart toward the things of God?

PRAYER FOR TODAY

Heavenly Father, prepare my heart so that it becomes good soil for your message to produce a large harvest. Help me to not become entangled with material things that can choke the spiritual life out of me. Lord, please use my life to bring other people into your kingdom. In Jesus' name I pray. Amen.

DAY 4

MARK 10:17–31

People with money seem to have a way of getting whatever they want. Wealth can purchase luxuries to please you, lawyers to keep you out of trouble, lobbyists to keep you in power, and luggage for you to travel the world. But one thing money cannot buy is eternal life, and without the promise of eternal life, there is very little in this life for which to live. In today's Scripture reading, Jesus meets a man who thought he could purchase eternal life.

Jesus had been in Judea teaching and ministering. As he was leaving Judea, a young man asked him, "What must I do to inherit eternal life?" (v. 17). Even though the young man was rich, he recognized there was more than this life. His question was sincere and honest, but it showed a lack of understanding about what Jesus had been teaching. The man had heard Jesus say, "Let the little children come to me, and do not hinder them, for the kingdom of God belongs to such as these. I tell you the truth, anyone who will not receive the kingdom of God like a little child will never enter it" (vv. 14–15). In spite of what Jesus had just said, the man was convinced there was something he had to do to receive the inheritance, or free gift, of eternal life.

Jesus, recognizing that this man was a religious man, told him he must keep the commandments, to which the man replied, "All these I have kept since I was a boy" (v. 20). The man was referring to the Jewish custom of bar mitzvah, which means "son of the commandments." When a Jewish boy turned thirteen, he assumed personal responsibility for obeying the commandments. At that age, he was accountable before the law and was on his way to becoming a man. The young man wasn't claiming to be perfect; rather, he was claiming to have done his best, since the age of thirteen, to keep the commandments.

Jesus did not doubt the young man's devotion, and in love, he spoke directly to the man's point of need. Jesus told him he needed to liquidate all his assets, give the money to the poor, and follow him (v. 21). Jesus was saying that anyone who wants to follow him has to be willing to give up what is most important, and to this young man, his money and possessions were more important, so "he went away sad" (v. 22). Eternal life is a gift that cannot be purchased because God doesn't want or need your money. He wants your entire life!

The largest animal in Palestine was the camel. In explaining to his disciples what had just happened, Jesus said, "It is easier for a camel to go through the eye of a needle than for a rich man to enter the kingdom of God" (v. 25). The disciples immediately understood the analogy and asked, "Who then can be saved?" (v. 26). Jesus replied, "With man this is impossible, but not with God; all things are possible with God" (v. 27).

Jesus was not condemning wealth, but the love of wealth and the dependence people put in their riches instead of him. Eternal life is a free gift of God, and only possible through faith in him. The rich man could not accept that fact. Can you? Are you willing to give up what is most important to you in order to follow Jesus?

QUESTIONS FOR REFLECTION

1. How does the promise of eternal life make this present life worth living? Do you agree or disagree with the statement that without the promise of eternal life there is really nothing in this life for which to live? Why or why not?

2. What do you think Jesus meant when he said it would be "easier for a camel to go through the eye of a needle than for a rich man to enter the kingdom of God" (v. 25)? Why do wealth and riches make it so difficult to believe in Jesus?

3. Are you willing to forsake what is most important to you in order to follow Jesus?

PRAYER FOR TODAY

Dear God, may I never put more trust and faith in money and things than I do in you. Thank you for loving me and for the truth that you have shown me. Lord, whatever it is that I value most, I gladly give that to you in order to follow you. In Jesus' name I pray. Amen.

DAY 5

Why do we equate riches with being blessed and poverty with being punished? I seldom hear people discuss how much God has blessed them when they have lost everything and have had to resort to begging on the streets to survive. But countless times I have heard the rich talk about how they have been blessed by God. The Bible neither condemns nor praises wealth. Likewise, the Bible neither condemns nor praises poverty. What the Bible praises is personal faith in God, and what the Bible condemns is a lack of faith in him.

Today's story is a contrast between a wealthy, unnamed man, and a poor beggar named Lazarus. The fact Jesus named the beggar makes it possible this was a real story based on a real person. The lives of the wealthy man and Lazarus could not have been more different. The only thing they had in common was they both lived and died. And as different as their lives were, so were their eternal destinations.

Lazarus was carried by angels to "Abraham's side" (v. 22), while the wealthy man died and went to hell "where he was in torment" (v. 23). "Abraham's side" was an expression used in the Talmud to describe heaven. Thus, in this story, the beggar was blessed while the privileged man was cursed. What each man possessed on earth carried no weight regarding what he received after death.

On earth, Lazarus was lucky if he received scraps from the rich man's table (v. 21); and now, the rich man begged for Lazarus to be given permission to give him a drop of water (v. 24). Abraham reminded the rich man of the difference in his and the beggar's earthly lives and their lives now; he explained that it would be impossible for Lazarus to do what the rich man requested (vv. 25–26).

The wealthy man then requested that Lazarus be given permission to go back to earth to warn the wealthy man's family about hell. Abraham said there was no need for that because the Old Testament has plenty of warnings if people would just listen (vv. 27–28). Then, in a prophetic statement about the resurrection of Jesus, Abraham said, "If they do not listen to Moses and the Prophets, they will not be convinced even if someone rises from the dead" (v. 31). Today, many people are looking for a miraculous sign to prove to them the reality of God, Jesus, heaven, and hell. But all a person needs to know has been written down in the Bible. If a person will not believe in the written Word of God, neither will that person believe in the supernatural work of God.

All week we have been studying the futility of chasing after wealth and possessions. The simple truth is you cannot buy your way into heaven, and those things that you can buy while on earth will not ultimately satisfy you in this life. More important than temporary stuff is eternal salvation, and there is only one way to receive God's free gift of eternal life. The Bible says "that if you confess with your mouth, 'Jesus is Lord,' and believe in your heart that God raised him from the dead, you will be saved. For it is with your heart that you believe and are justified, and it is with your mouth that you confess and are saved" (Rom. 10:9–10). "For it is by grace you have been saved, through faith—and this is not from yourselves, it is the gift of God—not by works [or riches and possessions], so that no one can boast" (Eph. 2:8–9).

Have you received God's free gift of eternal life through personal faith in Jesus Christ?

QUESTIONS FOR REFLECTION

1. Why do you think we consistently compare riches to being blessed and poverty to being punished?

2. Have you received God's free gift of eternal life through personal faith in Jesus Christ? If not, and you would like to, repeat the prayer below.

PRAYER FOR TODAY

Dear God, I admit that I am a sinner. I ask you to forgive me of my sins. Thank you for sending your Son, Jesus, to die on the cross for my sins. I surrender my life to you. I confess that Jesus is Lord. I believe you raised him from the dead. God, right now I commit my entire life to you. Come into my heart and take control. Thank you for your love, mercy, and grace. In Jesus' name I pray. Amen.

GIVE GENEROUSLY

While working his way through college, one of my friends was a security guard at a high-rise condominium. Every person who lived in the building was a millionaire; most were retired millionaires. Living in this building were some of the nicest people he had ever met, as well as some of the most miserable. My friend says that it was while working at this place that he started to truly understand that money cannot buy happiness. The difference, he said, was that people who had a lot of money and were satisfied with what they had were usually happy people; while people who had a lot of money and wanted more were usually unhappy people. To put it another way, the more generous a person was with what they had, the happier they were. The stingier a person was with what they had, the less likely they were to be happy. There is a reason the words *miser* and *miserable* are so similar.

Generosity is a large part of enjoying total quality finances. Generosity is also the subject of this week's study.

DAY 1

ACTS 2:42–47; 4:32–35

The most powerful force in all the earth is the local church when it is doing what it was created to do. The local church is to be to the world today what Jesus was to the world in his day. Jesus was God in human form. The church is Jesus in bodily form.

The church, as described in the book of Acts, turned their world upside down. They changed the culture, not by becoming part of the culture but by being countercultural. In one day after one sermon, the church grew from about one hundred fifty people to over three thousand people (see Acts 2:14–41). The first church wasn't perfect, but it was powerful. The message they preached and the lifestyle they lived attracted people to Jesus. One of the keys to their ability to impact their society was their generosity. In today's Scripture reading, we see their generosity, and learn that it grew out of their desire to worship God and love people.

Without buildings, programs, or budgets, the first believers gathered daily in each other's homes and in the temple courts to learn from the apostles, celebrate the Lord's Supper, and meet the needs of others. The early believers "had everything in common" (2:44) and "shared everything they had" (4:32), which shows the unselfishness and generosity that marked their lives. The first Christians did not live in a commune, pooling their resources and distributing them equally. But they did see their possessions as tools God had given them to meet the needs of others, and as such, they held on to their possessions lightly, not as owners of anything, but as stewards of everything. As needs were made known to the congregation, people would sell "their possessions and goods" (2:45), and "those who owned lands or houses sold them, brought the money from the sales and put it at the apostles' feet, and it was distributed to anyone as he had need" (4:34–35). As a result of their generosity, "there were no needy persons among them" (4:34).

The key for the church to grow is not another program or a new pastor. The key is for the people in the church to stop being miserable and start being generous and grateful. Notice what happened as the first church lived out their faith: "The Lord added to their number daily those who were being saved" (2:47).

QUESTIONS FOR REFLECTION

1. In what ways do you think generosity is a large part of enjoying total quality finances?

2. Do you agree with the statement, "The most powerful force in all the earth is the local church when it is doing what it was created to do"? Why or why not?

3. How generous do you consider yourself to be? Do you think you need to be more or less generous?

PRAYER FOR TODAY

Father God, you are gracious and generous. You showed your generosity by giving the best you had to offer—Jesus. Thank you so much. Teach me to be both gracious and generous. I pray for a spirit of generosity, not just in my life, but in the life of my church. In Jesus' name I pray. Amen.

DAY 2

MARK 12:41–44

There was once an elderly widow, who lived in an assisted living establishment and was no longer able to attend her church's services. She wasn't wealthy by any standard, but once a month, very faithfully, she mailed the church a ten dollar check. What does a church do with ten dollars? An elder in the church put this lovely lady's gift into perspective by saying, "You know, ten dollars is not a lot of money, but her ten dollars could be the very reason God has blessed us so we can pay our bills each month." He went on to add, "Her ten dollars could be the only thing keeping our doors open."

This wise elder based his comments on today's Scripture reading.

Jesus, teaching in the temple courts, was critical of the religious leaders of his day, stating they did what they did for show, not out of sincerity. Instead of helping people, Jesus said these leaders "devour widows' houses" (v. 40). Jesus then "sat down opposite the place where the offerings were put" (v. 41).

The place where offerings were collected was the "court of the women," located east of Herod's temple. Both men and women were allowed here, but women could go no farther into the temple buildings. Along the walls of the court were thirteen strategically positioned, trumpet-shaped receptacles where people were expected to place their offerings and donations to the temple. Jesus sat down opposite of these receptacles and watched as people gave their donations. The currency in Jesus' day were coins, and the larger the coin, the more money it represented and the more noise it made when placed in the receptacles. From his vantage point, Jesus could see and hear how much each person gave.

What caught Jesus' attention was not the wealthy who gave large amounts, but one widow who "put in two very small copper coins, worth only a fraction of a penny" (v. 42). Jesus commended the lady to his disciples because her gift was generous. The gift did not come out of her wealth, but out of her poverty. Jesus said she put in "all she had to live on" (v. 44). She did not give out of her abundance, but out of her need. And now she was relying on God for her next meal.

It is one thing to give, but it is another thing to be generous. You can give out of what has been given to you, but to be generous means to give sacrificially. It means giving to the point that you have to do without something. That type of giving is rare, but it is needed to demonstrate that all you have comes from God, and it is God who you are trusting to meet your needs. You can't be generous and greedy at the same time.

QUESTIONS FOR REFLECTION

1. What do you think is the difference between giving and being generous? How would you describe that difference to someone else?

2. Why do you think Jesus was more impressed by the widow's small gift as opposed to the wealthy person's large gift?

3. Have you ever given all you had to God so that you had to depend on him for your next meal?

PRAYER FOR TODAY

Dear God, thank you for the wonderful example the widow in today's Scripture reading gives me. Teach me to be sacrificially generous. Help me to overcome my greed and hold loosely all that you have given me. In Jesus' name I pray. Amen.

DAY 3

1 JOHN 3:16–24

How do you know a person who claims to be Christian is really a Christian? Is it because they go to church two or three times a week? Is it because they give money and do good deeds? Is it because they confess Jesus? Is it because they don't swear or drink? Is it because they love other people? How do you know a person is really a Christian? The primary trait that characterizes a disciple of Jesus is love—love for God and other people. But how do we know what love is, and how do we know we have love? In other words, how do we know we are Christians?

In today's Scripture reading, John gives us two tests to determine if a person who claims to be a Christian is really a Christian. One test you already know; the other may surprise you.

We know we have this love because we have obeyed God's "command: to believe in the name of his Son, Jesus Christ" (v. 23). This is the first test of a person's faith. "To believe" means to entrust, to put something into the care of another. To believe in Jesus means you have, by faith, placed your life into his hands because you know he is the Christ, God's Messiah. Because of our faith in Jesus Christ, we love others, and it is the Holy Spirit that gives us the ability to love others in the same way God has loved us.

By dying on the cross for our sins, Jesus epitomized love (v. 16). Likewise, "we ought to lay down our lives for our brothers" (v. 16). Here is the second test, the one that may surprise you. How do we sacrifice our lives for others, demonstrating our love for them? How do we "lay down our lives"? By being generous with what we have, sacrificially giving to help others in need (v. 17). The primary characteristic of a disciple of Jesus is love. We love God by placing our faith in Jesus Christ. We love others by our willingness to give our material possessions to those in need. Does this surprise you? You pass the test of being a true Christian by your willingness to sacrifice your possessions for those in need. "Dear children, let us not love with words or tongue but with actions and in truth" (v. 18).

QUESTIONS FOR REFLECTION

1. How do you know if a person who claims to be a Christian is really a Christian? Is this type of judging another person right or wrong? Why?

2. What were the two tests given in today's Scripture passage to tell if a person is truly a Christian? What is the primary characteristic of a disciple of Jesus?

3. In what ways should we be willing to "lay down our lives for our brothers" (v. 16)?

PRAYER FOR TODAY

Dear Jesus, thank you for dying for me. By doing so, you defined what true love really is. I pray I will learn to love you and others in the way that you love me. I pray for a willingness to give sacrificially to those who are in need. Thank you for filling me with your Holy Spirit. In Jesus' name I pray. Amen.

DAY 4

2 CORINTHIANS 9:6–15

Do you know the difference between compound interest and simple interest? Simple interest only pays interest on the principle of the investment. For example, if you invest ten thousand dollars at 10 percent simple annual interest, after one year, you will have eleven thousand dollars. At the end of fifteen years, you will have twenty-five thousand dollars. If, however, you invest ten thousand dollars at 10 percent compound annual interest, at the end of the first year, you will have eleven thousand dollars. But after fifteen years you will have 41,772 dollars. That's a difference of 16,772 dollars!

The law of compounding interest is much like the agricultural law of sowing and reaping that Paul used to make a point in today's Scripture reading. Paul used the law of sowing and reaping as an analogy for being generous. The more you sow, the more you reap. Likewise, the more generous you are, the more generously you will reap. You cannot out give God! God repays generosity, not with simple interest, but with compound interest. Knowing this to be true, "Each man should give what he has decided in his heart to give, not reluctantly or under compulsion, for God loves a cheerful giver" (v. 7).

Read verse 8. The key word in here is *all*. The more generous you are with what you have, the more dependent you are on God to supply your needs, and God will always supply all your needs. In the economic world, compound interest is determined by the market and can fluctuate drastically. In the spiritual world, compound interest, based on your generosity, is dependent on God, and God doesn't change.

The more generous you are, the more prosperous you will be, and the more prosperous you become, the more generous you will continue to be (v. 11). If you are willing to be generous, God will use you as a channel of blessings to others. The area of your prosperity, however, is in the spiritual realm, not necessarily in the physical. God promises to "enlarge the harvest of your righteousness" (v. 10), and you can't place a price tag on that type of harvest. It is far more valuable than earthly treasures.

Generosity can also lead to evangelism. Paul encouraged the believers in Corinth to continue being generous because their generosity overflowed in "many expressions of thanks to God" (v. 12), and because of their generosity, "men will praise God" (v. 13). Your generosity can make an eternal difference in someone else's life.

Don't ever stop being generous, because you serve an even more generous God.

QUESTIONS FOR REFLECTION

1. How would you explain the relationship of generosity through the laws of compounding interest and sowing and reaping?

2. In what ways do you think God promises to make a generous person prosperous? Be specific if you can.

3. How do you see generosity leading to evangelism?

PRAYER FOR TODAY

Lord, help me to be more generous. I pray you will change my heart into a cheerful giver and that I will learn to give more than I can even imagine right now. You are generous, and I want to be like you. In Jesus' name I pray. Amen.

DAY 5

MATTHEW 6:1–4

Have you walked through a college or university campus lately? If not, sometime soon take the time to do so and notice the names on all the different buildings. Many college and university buildings are named after people who gave large donations for the completion of that building. While walking through the campus, notice the landscape and look closely. Chances are you will find plaques stating who gave the money for that particular tree, or koi pond, or park bench. People like to give to things they think will carry on their legacy or the name of their family. It is human nature to want to be recognized for your generosity.

Certainly there's a place for desiring recognition, but according to Jesus' words in today's Scripture reading, there is no place for desiring recognition when it comes to being generous to the poor.

Jesus says that our motivation for doing good deeds should not be public recognition. If admiration is what you are after, then admiration is the only reward you will receive. There are all types of different ways to do good, but the one way Jesus chooses as an example is doing good by giving to the needy.

Jesus assumes we will give to the needy. When you do give, don't make a big production out of it. "Do not announce it with trumpets" (v. 2). Another way of saying this is, "Don't toot your own horn." Don't give to the needy to gain the praise of other people or to be recognized for your generosity. Give to the needy because they need help and it is the right thing to do.

Jesus says that giving to the needy is to be so secretive and regular that you barely even know you are giving anymore—"Do not let your left hand know what your right hand is doing" (v. 3). The only recognition that should motivate us to give generously is that God will see what you have done and "will reward you" (v. 4). This is so hard to do, but when giving, especially for individual, specific needs, the more anonymous you can be, the better.

When we learn to hold on to stuff lightly and be generous with what we have, we will learn the true meaning of financial freedom. Generous giving is a crucial key to enjoying total quality financial life. It is through blessing others that we are blessed. Practice generosity, and watch how God blesses you.

QUESTIONS FOR REFLECTION

1. Is it always wrong to be recognized for your generosity? Why or why not? When is it OK, and when is it wrong?

2. Why do you think Jesus stressed secrecy so much in giving to the needy?

PRAYER FOR TODAY

Heavenly Father, I have grown so much, and I pray for the power to implement what I have learned. Show me the areas of my life that need to change. Open my eyes so that I can see the needs of people around me. Open my heart so that I will give as you have empowered me. In Jesus' name I pray. Amen.

I would love to volunteer at the homeless shelter, but I just don't have the time."

"I wish I could help you coach Little League baseball, but it doesn't fit in my schedule."

"I would teach the second grade Sunday school class at church, but with everything else I'm involved in, I can't right now."

"I know getting involved in my child's school is important, but I don't know when I would do it."

"If I had time I would . . ."

In our society, time is money, so you can't discuss total quality finances without discussing how you spend your time. Managing your time involves giving some of your time away to meet the needs of others. Next to managing your money, managing your time may be the most important thing you can do to experience total quality finances.

DAY 1

While everyone has a different amount of financial resources available to them, no one has more or less time than anyone else. We all have twenty-four hours a day, seven days a week, and three hundred sixty-five days a year. How you spend your time depends on what is important to you. As a follower of Jesus Christ, the most important thing is to love God by loving others. Thus, giving your time and doing good deeds is extremely important. Jesus alludes to the importance of doing good in today's Scripture reading.

Jesus uses two analogies to emphasize the importance and effects of giving your time to do good works. The first analogy is "salt" (v. 13). In the same way that salt purifies, preserves, and protects food from spoiling, so our lives are to impact our communities for good. Probably, the salt Jesus was referring to came from the Dead Sea, which is nine times saltier than the oceans. In addition to being used to preserve and season food, salt was also used by Jews in worship and by doctors for different medical purposes. For example, newborn babies were often rubbed in salt, since it was believed that salt promoted good health (see Ezek. 16:4). Sometimes salt was used to pay Roman soldiers; in fact, it is the root of the English word *salary*. But when salt, especially salt from the Dead Sea, lost its saltiness, the only thing it was good for was to be thrown outside and used like gravel. The Roman army would often use this unsalted salt to make their enemies' land barren. The point Jesus was making is that we are to live our lives in such a way as to positively impact our surroundings.

When we don't live that way, there really is no sense in claiming to be his disciples.

The second analogy Jesus uses is "light" (vv. 14–16). The primary purpose of light is to give direction. When people turn on a light, they don't do so to hide something, but to point out something. The lamp Jesus referred to was a small clay lamp that burned olive oil drawn up by a wick. These lamps only gave out a modest amount of light, and so they were strategically placed in homes to give maximum benefit. The lamp stand was often a niche built into the wall of a home so that the lamp could safely burn all night. Jesus' point is that regardless of how bright our lights may be—how much good we think we are doing—we are to continue to do good; we are to continue to give our time and serve others so that people "may see your good deeds and praise your Father in heaven" (v. 16).

QUESTIONS FOR REFLECTION

1. What do you think is the connection between managing your money and time? Do you think there is a connection?

2. What do you think Jesus meant by saying we "are the salt of the earth" (v. 13)? How would you describe what he meant to someone else? What about "the light of the world" (v. 14)? How would you describe this to someone else?

3. Which analogy makes the most sense to you—salt of the earth or light of the world? Why?

PRAYER FOR TODAY

Dear Jesus, I want to live a life that is pleasing to you. I want to make a difference in my family and community for you. I commit my life to you. I pray you will transform me into salt and light. I pray I will never lose my saltiness and never hide my light. In Jesus' name I pray. Amen.

DAY 2

LUKE 10:25–37

Have you ever sped by a person who was stuck on the side of the road with a flat tire? Have you ever hurried up to get in front of a person going through the checkout line at the grocery store?

I have been guilty of doing both of those things and have rationalized it, because I didn't have time or I didn't want to get involved or I thought someone else would help. In reality, the reason I didn't help or the reason I didn't let the other person go first is because I didn't want to waste my time. I thought I had more important things to do. In today's Scripture reading, Jesus tells a story that is similar to the situations I just described. Jesus was responding to a question asked by an "expert in the law" (v. 25). The question was, "What must I do to inherit eternal life?" (v. 25). Jesus asked the lawyer what he thought the answer was, to which the lawyer replied, "'Love the Lord your God with all your heart and with all your soul and with all your strength and with all your mind'; and, 'Love your neighbor as yourself'" (v. 27). Jesus remarked that he had answered correctly. Then, the lawyer asked another question, "Who is my neighbor?" (v. 29). It was in answering that question that Jesus told the story.

The story was about a man who went on a seventeen-mile journey from Jerusalem to Jericho. The road between the two cities descended from about twenty-five hundred feet above sea level to about eight hundred feet below sea level and ran though rocky, desert terrain. Because of the rural nature of this road, it was notorious for hiding thieves and robbers and dangerous to travel on alone.

While on his way to Jericho, the man was robbed, beaten, and left for dead. While he was lying there beside the road, three people passed by. The first two were religious people, a priest and a Levite. Since both the priest and the Levite were Jewish, you might assume they would help their fellow countryman, but neither one of them stopped to help. The third person was a Samaritan. Samaritans and Jews despised each other. The Jews considered the Samaritans to be half-breeds, and the Samaritans resented the Jews for their piousness. It is no accident that Jesus made the Samaritan, the one least expected to help, the hero in the story. The Samaritan offered immediate help to the man and then made sure he would be taken care of after he left. The Samaritan went above and beyond what would have been expected of him. He gave his time and money to help the Jew get back on his feet.

The point of Jesus' story is that everyone and anyone who has a need is your neighbor, regardless of race, color, or creed. At all times, we are to be willing to give our time and resources to help our neighbor.

QUESTIONS FOR REFLECTION

1. If someone were to ask you how they could have eternal life, how would you answer them?

2. According to Jesus' story, who is your neighbor? Are you willing to give your time and resources to help him or her?

PRAYER FOR TODAY

Heavenly Father, help me to see anyone who has a need as my neighbor. Create in me a desire to give of my time and resources to help other people. Thank you for the changes you are making in my life. In Jesus' name I pray. Amen.

DAY 3

※

ECCLESIASTES 3:1–15

If time were money, then maybe seconds would be pennies. Every day has 86,400 seconds. If those seconds were pennies, it would equal 864 dollars. If time was money, every day you have 864 dollars to spend, or six thousand dollars per week, or 315,000 dollars per year. If time was money, you would have to spend every penny every day. What you didn't spend would be forfeited, and what you did spend could be spent only once. If time really was money, how would you spend it?

Time is the only thing that is truly equal for all people. How we spend our time is based on our priorities. But regardless of how you choose to spend it, today's Scripture reading says there is a time for everything.

In verses 2–8, Solomon listed fourteen pairs of things that encompass nearly every aspect of life. Notice how the pairs cancel each other out. For example, Solomon wrote, "a time to be born and a time to die" (v. 2), "a time to kill and a time to heal" (v. 3), "a time to love and a time to hate, a time for war and a time for peace" (v. 8). Taken as a whole, Solomon saw life as a series of events. He saw life as a continual cycle, always moving, always changing, but always remaining the same.

From a human perspective, Solomon concluded that life is meaningless, like chasing after the wind. However, from a spiritual perspective, nothing is further from the truth. Solomon said that God has made everything "beautiful in its time" (v. 11). Furthermore, God has set in the hearts of man a longing for more than this life.

Something within us says there is more to life than just this life. Something within us longs for eternity. Solomon concluded, "I know that there is nothing better for men than to be happy and to do good while they live. . . . This is the gift of God" (vv. 12–13). When we understand that life is more than what is going on right now—when we understand there is an eternal dimension to life—that understanding gives this life a purpose, and part of that purpose is giving your time doing good for others. Life is better when we live it to the fullest by serving other people more than ourselves.

When you get down and discouraged about life and how it has turned out or not turned out, the best way to get out of that depressed state is to look outside of yourself, give your time, and serve someone else. Try volunteering your time doing good. You will not be sorry.

QUESTIONS FOR REFLECTION

1. Look over the fourteen pairs listed in verses 2–8. Solomon uses these pairs to say there is a time for everything. How do the pairs cancel each other out? What does their canceling each other out say about time? Can you think of a pair you would add?

2. How does recognizing there is more to this life make life worth living?

PRAYER FOR TODAY

Lord, there is always time to do good. Help me take that time and look for ways to serve others. Thank you for making everything beautiful in its time. In Jesus' name I pray. Amen.

DAY 4

JAMES 4:13–17

Time management is essential to living a total quality life. Planning is important in order to be effective in your daily routine. But planning that leaves God out is dangerous. Planning as if God doesn't exist is even more dangerous. In today's Scripture reading, James warns us against such hazardous planning.

At first glance, it may appear James is condemning any type of wise planning. But that is not his point. What he is condemning is unwise planning, and unwise planning is planning that leaves out God. He tells us it is futile to plan what you are going to do tomorrow or the next day, because you don't have any way of knowing what will happen then. You may have big plans for tomorrow, but you could die during the night, or some other type of emergency may take place that changes your plans. After all, "What is your life? You are a mist that appears for a little while and then vanishes" (v. 14). It is futile to plan, because doing so deceives you into thinking you are somehow in control, and ultimately you are not in control.

Wise planning has a spiritual component to it. Wise planning says, "This is what we would like to do tomorrow, if God permits." This type of planning includes God, and acknowledges that, ultimately, he is sovereign and in control. That one simple phrase, "If it is the Lord's will" (v. 15), keeps all of life in perspective because it is a constant reminder of who is really in charge.

When we think we are in charge and hurry and hustle to make a living, we are tempted to boast and brag. James writes, "All such boasting is evil" (v. 16). But again, when we pray for God's will to be done, we recognize that all we have comes from him, and that is the proper perspective we need to have about life.

Verse 17 applies to many situations. As a follower of Jesus, when we are shown something in God's Word or when the Spirit gives us insight into what we should do, if we don't do it, we have sinned. This is called the sin of omission—sinning by not doing something. When God shows you what you should do, the best response is to humbly submit and obey.

QUESTIONS FOR REFLECTION

1. How do you balance good, practical, business planning with God's oversight of all things?

2. Why do you think James said "all such boasting is evil" (v. 16)? How is boasting evil?

3. How do you think recognizing God's authority keeps life in perspective?

PRAYER FOR TODAY

Dear God, I believe you are over all things, and I trust in your authority. In the past, I have made plans without thinking about you and what you want me to do. Forgive me for thinking I am somehow in control. May I boast and brag only of you. In Jesus' name I pray. Amen.

DAY 5

❧

ECCLESIASTES 12:9–14

Have you heard the saying, "The main thing is to keep the main thing the main thing"? Most of life's trouble comes when we get sidetracked on one issue or another, and the main thing is no longer the main thing. One of the things that can sidetrack us is money. Money is never to be the main thing. When money becomes the main thing, we lose focus on what is really important.

What, then, is the main thing? Solomon, one of the wisest men ever, tells us what the main thing should be in today's Scripture reading.

Solomon set out to find the meaning and purpose of life, while initially leaving out God. The book of Ecclesiastes is his journal of what he discovered. Solomon's conclusion was that apart from God, all of life is meaningless. Apart from God, there is no main thing. Why not? Because God is the main thing.

If you want to enjoy total quality life, listen to Solomon's words. He wrote, "The words of the wise are like goads, their collected sayings like firmly embedded nails—given by one Shepherd" (v. 11). Goads and nails are two tools of the shepherd. A goad is a tool used to prod and motivate reluctant sheep forward; nails are used to secure fences, keeping sheep from wandering. Through words of wisdom, our Good Shepherd prods us along and keeps us safe, if we will only listen and apply what we hear.

Solomon closed his journal with the best piece of advice anyone could ever give or receive. His advice can be applied to finances or to spending our time wisely. In his advice, he tells us what the main thing is: "Now all has been heard; here is the conclusion of the matter: Fear God and keep his commandments, for this is the whole duty of man" (v. 13).

The purpose of life is summarized by the phrase, "Fear God and keep his commandments." To fear God means to respect him and to live in awe of who he is. The best way to show our reverential fear is by keeping God's commandments. The Great Commandment is to love God and love one another. That is the main thing, and when it comes to giving our time and finances, we must keep the main thing the main thing. "For God will bring every deed into judgment, including every hidden thing, whether it is good or evil" (v. 14).

QUESTIONS FOR REFLECTION

1. What are some minor things that people place in their lives that interfere with the main thing?

2. What steps can you take this week to keep the main thing the main thing?

3. What do you think it means to "fear God and keep his commandments" (v. 13)? Why should this be the main thing? How would you explain what this means to someone else?

PRAYER FOR TODAY

Dear Lord, I pray my life will never be the same because of what I have read, studied, and learned from your Word these past six weeks. You are a faithful and merciful God. You have filled me with your Holy Spirit. I pray I will use my finances and time wisely and for your glory. In Jesus' name I pray. Amen.